SONNETS
FROM THE
PORTUGUESE
AND OTHER LOVE POEMS

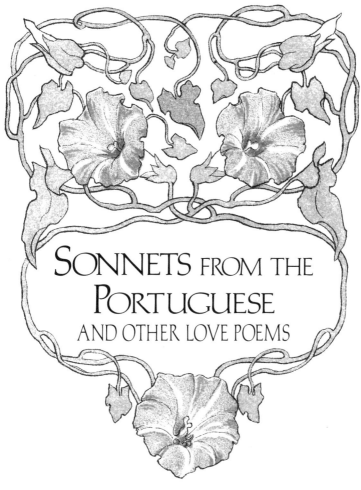

Sonnets from the Portuguese
and other love poems

Elizabeth Barrett Browning

Illustrated by Margaret Armstrong

GRAMERCY BOOKS
NEW YORK

Introduction copyright © 1993 by Random House Value Publishing, Inc.

This edition is published by Gramercy Books,
a division of Random House Value Publishing, Inc.,
201 East 50th Street, New York, New York 10022.

Gramercy Books and colophon are trademarks of
Random House Value Publishing, Inc.

Random House
New York • Toronto • London • Sydney • Auckland
http://www.randomhouse.com/

Printed and bound in Singapore

A CIP catalog record for this book is available from the Library of Congress.

Sonnets from the Portuguese and Other Love Poems / by Elizabeth Barrett Browning /
illustrated by Margaret Armstrong
ISBN 0-517-18721-3

8 7 6 5 4 3 2

CONTENTS

INTRODUCTION

The relationship of Elizabeth Barrett and Robert Browning, from their first meeting in January 1845, resulted in some of the most wonderful love poems ever written in the English language. Until her marriage, Elizabeth Barrett, who had been frail in health since a riding accident at the age of fifteen, had lived for forty years under the despotic rule of her father.

She began to write verse when she was very young, and *The Battle of Marathon* was privately published by her father when she was only fourteen years old. Although Robert Browning's career had begun in 1835, with the publication of *Paracelsus,* by the time Elizabeth Barrett met him she had published three more collections of poems and was far more famous than he.

The couple married on September 12, 1846, against her father's wishes, and fled to Italy where they lived until her death in 1861. She was never reconciled with her family, but during these years, Elizabeth Barrett Browning's fame as a poet grew, culminating in her highly successful "novel-poem" *Aurora Leigh,* published in 1856.

A few years after their marriage, Robert Browning was shown the forty-four love sonnets that his wife had written in secret before and after their marriage. He encouraged her to publish them, and in 1850 *Sonnets from the Portuguese* appeared as part of the revised two-volume edition of her *Poems.* Browning affectionately called her his "Portuguese," because of her olive complexion, and it was from this pet name, as well as from her desire to intimate that these intensely personal poems had been adapted from another language, that the unusual title was derived.

Along with *Sonnets from the Portuguese,* this edition includes six additional poignant and exquisite love poems. Elizabeth Barrett Browning's timeless verses are complemented by the beautiful decorative floral borders of the early twentieth-century American book designer and illustrator Margaret Armstrong.

GAIL HARVEY

New York

SONNETS
FROM
THE
PORTUGUESE

I

I thought once how Theocritus had sung
Of the sweet years, the dear and wished-for years,
Who each one in a gracious hand appears
To bear a gift for mortals, old or young:
And, as I mused it in his antique tongue,
I saw, in gradual vision through my tears,
The sweet, sad years, the melancholy years,
Those of my own life, who by turns had flung
A shadow across me. Straightway I was 'ware,
So weeping, how a mystic Shape did move
Behind me, and drew me backward by the hair;
And a voice said in mastery, while I strove,—
"Guess now who holds thee!"—"Death," I said,
    But there,
The silver answer rang,—"Not Death, but Love."

II

But only three in all God's universe
Have heard this word thou hast said,—Himself, beside
Thee speaking, and me listening! and replied
One of us . . . *that* was God . . . and laid the curse
So darkly on my eyelids, as to amerce
My sight from seeing thee,—that if I had died,
The death-weights, placed there, would have signified
Less absolute exclusion. "Nay" is worse
From God than from all others, O my friend!
Men could not part us with their worldly jars,
Nor the seas change us, nor the tempests bend;
Our hands would touch for all the mountain-bars.—
And, heaven being rolled between us at the end,
We should but vow the faster for the stars.

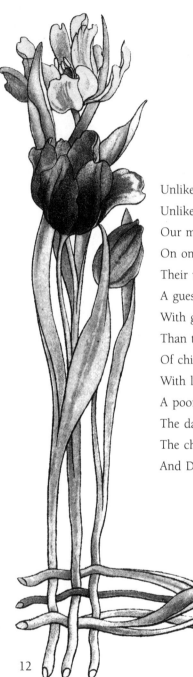

III

Unlike are we, unlike, O princely Heart!
Unlike our uses and our destinies.
Our ministering two angels look surprise
On one another, as they strike athwart
Their wings in passing. Thou, bethink thee, art
A guest for queens to social pageantries,
With gages from a hundred brighter eyes
Than tears even can make mine, to play thy part
Of chief musician. What hast *thou* to do
With looking from the lattice-lights at me,
A poor, tired, wandering singer, . . . singing throug
The dark, and leaning up a cypress tree?
The chrism is on thine head, on mine, the dew,—
And Death must dig the level where these agree.

IV

Thou hast thy calling to some palace-floor,
Most gracious singer of high poems! where
The dancers will break footing, from the care
Of watching up thy pregnant lips for more.
And dost thou lift this house's latch too poor
For hand of thine? and canst thou think and bear
To let thy music drop here unaware
In folds of golden fullness at my door?
Look up and see the casement broken in,
The bats and owlets builders in the roof!
My cricket chirps against thy mandolin.
Hush, call no echo up in further proof
Of desolation! there's a voice within
That weeps . . . as thou must sing . . . alone, aloof.

V

I lift my heavy heart up solemnly,
As once Electra her sepulchral urn,
And, looking in thine eyes, I overturn
The ashes at thy feet. Behold and see
What a great heap of grief lay hid in me,
And how the red wild sparkles dimly burn
Through the ashen grayness. If thy foot in scorn
Could tread them out to darkness utterly,
It might be well perhaps. But if instead
Thou wait beside me for the wind to blow
The gray dust up . . . those laurels on thine head,
O my Belovèd, will not shield thee so,
That none of all the fires shall scorch and shred
The hair beneath. Stand farther off then! go.

VI

Go from me. Yet I feel that I shall stand
Henceforward in thy shadow. Nevermore
Alone upon the threshold of my door
Of individual life, I shall command
The uses of my soul, nor lift my hand
Serenely in the sunshine as before,
Without the sense of that which I forbore—
Thy touch upon the palm. The widest land
Doom takes to part us, leaves thy heart in mine
With pulses that beat double. What I do
And what I dream include thee, as the wine
Must taste of its own grapes. And when I sue
God for myself, He hears that name of thine,
And sees within my eyes the tears of two.

VII

The face of all the world is changed, I think,
Since first I heard the footsteps of thy soul
Move still, oh, still, beside me, as they stole
Betwixt me and the dreadful outer brink
Of obvious death, where I, who thought to sink,
Was caught up into love, and taught the whole
Of life in a new rhythm. The cup of dole
God gave for baptism, I am fain to drink,
And praise its sweetness, Sweet, with thee anear.
The names of country, heaven, are changed away
For where thou art or shalt be, there or here;
And this . . . this lute and song . . . loved yesterd.
(The singing angels know) are only dear
Because thy name moves right in what they say.

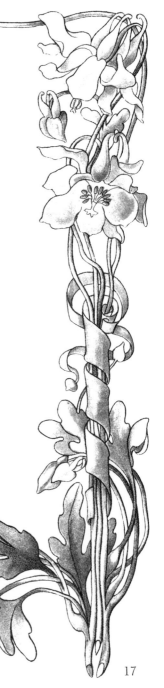

VIII

What can I give thee back, O liberal
And princely giver, who hast brought the gold
And purple of thine heart, unstained, untold,
And laid them on the outside of the wall
For such as I to take or leave withal,
In unexpected largesse? am I cold,
Ungrateful, that for these most manifold
High gifts, I render nothing back at all?
Not so; not cold,—but very poor instead.
Ask God who knows. For frequent tears have run
The colors from my life, and left so dead
And pale a stuff, if it were not fitly done
To give the same as pillow to thy head.
Go farther! let it serve to trample on.

IX

Can it be right to give what I can give?
To let thee sit beneath the fall of tears
As salt as mine, and hear the sighing years
Re-sighing on my lips renunciative
Through those infrequent smiles which fail to live
For all thy adjurations? O my fears,
That this can scarce be right! We are not peers,
So to be lovers; and I own, and grieve,
That givers of such gifts as mine are, must
Be counted with the ungenerous. Out, alas!
I will not soil thy purple with my dust,
Nor breathe my poison on thy Venice-glass,
Nor give thee any love, which were unjust.
Belovèd, I only love thee! let it pass.

X

Yet, love, mere love, is beautiful indeed
And worthy of acceptation. Fire is bright,
Let temple burn, or flax; an equal light
Leaps in the flame from cedar-plank or weed.
And love is fire. And when I say at need
I love thee . . . mark! . . . *I love thee*—in thy sight
I stand transfigured, glorified aright,
With conscience of the new rays that proceed
Out of my face toward thine. There's nothing low
In love, when love the lowest: meanest creatures
Who love God, God accepts while loving so.
And what I *feel,* across the inferior features
Of what I *am,* doth flash itself, and show
How that great work of Love enhances Nature's.

XI

And therefore if to love can be desert,
I am not all unworthy. Cheeks as pale
As these you see, and trembling knees that fail
To bear the burden of a heavy heart,—
This weary minstrel-life that once was girt
To climb Aornus, and can scarce avail
To pipe now 'gainst the valley nightingale
A melancholy music,—why advert
To these things? O Belovèd, it is plain
I am not of thy worth nor for thy place!
And yet, because I love thee, I obtain
From that same love this vindicating grace,
To live on still in love, and yet in vain, . . .
To bless thee, yet renounce thee to thy face.

XII

Indeed this very love which is my boast,
And which, when rising up from breast to brow,
Doth crown me with a ruby large enow
To draw men's eyes and prove the inner cost, . . .
This love even, all my worth, to the uttermost,
I should not love withal, unless that thou
Hadst set me an example, shown me how,
When first thine earnest eyes with mine were crossed
And love called love. And thus, I cannot speak
Of love even, as a good thing of my own.
Thy soul hath snatched up mine all faint and weak
And placed it by thee on a golden throne,—
And that I love (O soul, we must be meek!)
Is by thee only, whom I love alone.

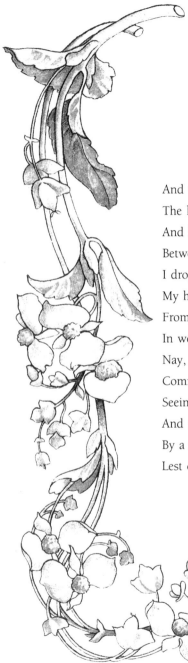

XIII

And wilt thou have me fashion into speech
The love I bear thee, finding words enough,
And hold the torch out, while the winds are rough
Between our faces, to cast light on each?—
I drop it at thy feet. I cannot teach
My hand to hold my spirit so far off
From myself—me—that I should bring thee proof
In words, of love hid in me out of reach.
Nay, let the silence of my womanhood
Commend my woman-love to thy belief,—
Seeing that I stand unwon, however wooed,
And rend the garment of my life, in brief,
By a most dauntless, voiceless fortitude,
Lest one touch of this heart convey its grief.

XIV

If thou must love me, let it be for nought
Except for love's sake only. Do not say
"I love her for her smile—her look—her way
Of speaking gently, . . . for a trick of thought
That falls in well with mine, and certes brought
A sense of pleasant ease on such a day"—
For these things in themselves, Belovèd, may
Be changed, or change for thee,—and love,
  so wrought.
May be unwrought so. Neither love me for
Thine own dear pity's wiping my cheeks dry,—
A creature might forget to weep, who bore
Thy comfort long, and lose thy love thereby!
But love me for love's sake, that evermore
Thou may'st love on, through love's eternity.

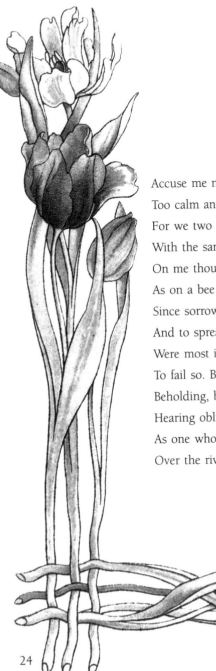

XV

Accuse me not, beseech thee, that I wear
Too calm and sad a face in front of thine;
For we two look two ways, and cannot shine
With the same sunlight on our brow and hair.
On me thou lookest with no doubting care,
As on a bee shut in a crystalline,—
Since sorrow hath shut me safe in love's divine,
And to spread wing and fly in the outer air
Were most impossible failure, if I strove
To fail so. But I look on thee—on thee—
Beholding, besides love, the end of love,
Hearing oblivion beyond memory!
As one who sits and gazes from above,
Over the rivers to the bitter sea.

XVI

And yet, because thou overcomest so,
Because thou art more noble and like a king,
Thou canst prevail against my fears and fling
Thy purple round me, till my heart shall grow
Too close against thine heart henceforth to know
How it shook when alone. Why, conquering
May prove as lordly and complete a thing
In lifting upward, as in crushing low!
And as a vanquished soldier yields his sword
To one who lifts him from the bloody earth,—
Even so, Belovèd, I at last record,
Here ends my strife. If *thou* invite me forth,
I rise above abasement at the word.
Make thy love larger to enlarge my worth!

XVII

My poet, thou canst touch on all the notes
God set between His After and Before,
And strike up and strike off the general roar
Of the rushing worlds a melody that floats
In a serene air purely. Antidotes
Of medicated music, answering for
Mankind's forlornest uses, thou canst pour
From thence into their ears. God's will devotes
Thine to such ends, and mine to wait on thine.
How, Dearest, wilt thou have me for most use?
A hope, to sing by gladly? . . . or a fine
Sad memory, with thy songs to interfuse?
A shade, in which to sing . . . or palm or pine?
A grave, on which to rest from singing? . . . Choose.

XVIII

I never gave a lock of hair away
To a man, Dearest, except this to thee,
Which now upon my fingers thoughtfully
I ring out to the full brown length and say
"Take it." My day of youth went yesterday;
My hair no longer bounds to my foot's glee,
Nor plant I it from rose- or myrtle-tree,
As girls do, any more. It only may
Now shade on two pale cheeks the mark of tears,
Taught drooping from the head that hangs aside
Through sorrow's trick. I thought the funeral-shears
Would take this first, but Love is justified,—
Take it thou, . . . finding pure, from all those years,
The kiss my mother left here when she died.

XIX

The soul's Rialto hath its merchandise;
I barter curl for curl upon that mart,
And from my poet's forehead to my heart
Receive this lock which outweighs argosies,—
As purely black, as erst to Pindar's eyes
The dim purpureal tresses gloomed athwart
The nine white Muse-brows. For this counterpart, .
The bay-crown's shade, Belovèd, I surmise,
Still lingers on thy curl, it is so black!
Thus, with a fillet of smooth-kissing breath,
I tie the shadows safe from gliding back
And lay the gift where nothing hindereth,
Here on my heart, as on thy brow, to lack
No natural heat till mine grows cold in death.

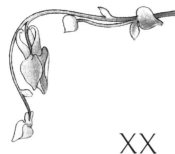

XX

Belovèd, my Belovèd, when I think
That thou wast in the world a year ago,
What time I sat alone here in the snow
And saw no footprint, heard the silence sink
No moment at thy voice, . . . but, link by link,
Went counting all my chains as if that so
They never could fall off at any blow
Struck by thy possible hand . . . why, thus I drink
Of life's great cup of wonder! Wonderful
Never to feel thee thrill the day or night
With personal act or speech,—nor ever cull
Some prescience of thee with the blossoms white
Thou sawest growing! Atheists are as dull,
Who cannot guess God's presence out of sight.

XXI

Say over again, and yet once over again,
That thou dost love me. Though the word repeated
Should seem "a cuckoo-song," as thou dost treat it,
Remember, never to the hill or plain,
Valley and wood, without her cuckoo-strain,
Comes the fresh Spring in all her green completed.
Belovèd, I, amid the darkness greeted
By a doubtful spirit-voice, in that doubt's pain
Cry, . . . "Speak once more . . . thou lovest!"
    Who can fear
Too many stars, though each in heaven shall roll,—
Too many flowers, though each shall crown the year?
Say thou dost love me, love me, love me—toll
The silver iterance!—only minding, Dear,
To love me also in silence with thy soul.

XXII

When our two souls stand up erect and strong,
Face to face, silent, drawing nigh and nigher,
Until the lengthening wings break into fire
At either curvèd point,—what bitter wrong
Can the earth do to us, that we should not long
Be here contented? Think! In mounting higher,
The angels would press on us and aspire
To drop some golden orb of perfect song
Into our deep, dear silence. Let us stay
Rather on earth, Belovèd,—where the unfit
Contrarious moods of men recoil away
And isolate pure spirits, and permit
A place to stand and love in for a day,
With darkness and the death-hour rounding it.

XXIII

Is it indeed so? If I lay here dead,
Wouldst thou miss any life in losing mine?
And would the sun for thee more coldly shine
Because of grave-damps falling round my head?
I marveled, my Belovèd, when I read
Thy thought so in the letter. I am thine—
But . . . *so* much to thee? Can I pour thy wine
While my hands tremble? Then my soul, instead
Of dreams of death, resumes life's lower range.
Then, love me, Love! Look on me—breathe on me!
As brighter ladies do not count it strange,
For love, to give up acres and degree,
I yield the grave for thy sake, and exchange
My near sweet view of heaven, for earth with thee!

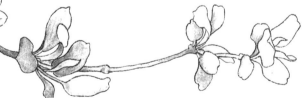

XXIV

Let the world's sharpness, like a clasping knife,
Shut in upon itself and do no harm
In this close hand of Love, now soft and warm,
And let us hear no sound of human strife
After the click of the shutting. Life to life—
I lean upon thee, Dear, without alarm,
And feel as safe as guarded by a charm
Against the stab of worldlings, who if rife
Are weak to injure. Very whitely still
The lilies of our lives may reassure
Their blossoms from their roots, accessible
Alone to heavenly dews that drop not fewer:
Growing straight, out of man's reach, on the hill.
God only, who made us rich, can make us poor.

XXV

A heavy heart, Belovèd, have I borne
From year to year until I saw thy face,
And sorrow after sorrow took the place
Of all those natural joys as lightly worn
As the stringed pearls, . . . each lifted in its turn
By a beating heart at dance-time. Hopes apace
Were changed to long despairs, till God's own grace
Could scarcely lift above the world forlorn
My heavy heart. Then *thou* didst bid me bring
And let it drop adown thy calmly great
Deep being! Fast it sinketh, as a thing
Which its own nature does precipitate,
While thine doth close above it, mediating
Betwixt the stars and the unaccomplished fate.

XXVI

I lived with visions for my company
Instead of men and women, years ago,
And found them gentle mates, nor thought to know
A sweeter music than they played to me.
But soon their trailing purple was not free
Of this world's dust,—their lutes did silent grow,
And I myself grew faint and blind below
Their vanishing eyes. Then THOU didst come . . . to be,
Belovèd, what they seemed. Their shining fronts,
Their songs, their splendors, (better, yet the same,
As river-water hallowed into fonts)
Met in thee, and from out thee overcame
My soul with satisfaction of all wants—
Because God's gifts put man's best dreams to shame.

XXVII

My own Belovèd, who has lifted me
From this drear flat of earth where I was thrown,
And, in betwixt the languid ringlets, blown
A life-breath, till the forehead hopefully
Shines out again, as all the angels see,
Before thy saving kiss! My own, my own,
Who camest to me when the world was gone,
And I who looked for only God, found *thee!*
I find thee; I am safe, and strong, and glad.
As one who stands in dewless asphodel,
Looks backward on the tedious time he had
In the upper life,—so I, with bosom-swell,
Make witness, here, between the good and bad,
That Love, as strong as Death, retrieves as well.

XXVIII

My letters! all dead paper, . . . mute and white!
And yet they seem alive and quivering
Against my tremulous hands which loose the string
And let them drop down on my knee tonight.
This said, . . . he wished to have me in his sight
Once, as a friend: this fixed a day in spring
To come and touch my hand . . . a simple thing,
Yet I wept for it!—this, . . . the paper's light . . .
Said, *Dear, I love thee*; and I sank and quailed
As if God's future thundered on my past.
This said, *I am thine*—and so its ink has paled
With lying at my heart that beat too fast.
And this . . . O Love, thy words have ill availed
If, what this said, I dared repeat at last!

XXIX

I think of thee!—my thoughts do twine and bud
About thee, as wild vines, about a tree,
Put out broad leaves, and soon there's nought to see
Except the straggling green which hides the wood.
Yet, O my palm-tree, be it understood
I will not have my thoughts instead of thee
Who art dearer, better! Rather, instantly
Renew thy presence; as a strong tree should,
Rustle thy boughs and set thy trunk all bare,
And let these bands of greenery which insphere thee,
Drop heavily down,—burst, shattered everywhere!
Because, in this deep joy to see and hear thee
And breathe within thy shadow a new air,
I do not think of thee—I am too near thee.

XXX

I see thine image through my tears tonight,
And yet today I saw thee smiling. How
Refer the cause?—Belovèd, is it thou
Or I, who makes me sad? The acolyte
Amid the chanted joy and thankful rite
May so fall flat, with pale insensate brow,
On the altar-stair. I hear thy voice and vow,
Perplexed, uncertain, since thou art out of sight,
As he, in his swooning ears, the choir's amen.
Belovèd, dost thou love? or did I see all
The glory as I dreamed, and fainted when
Too vehement light dilated my ideal,
For my soul's eyes? Will that light come again,
As now these tears come . . . falling hot and real?

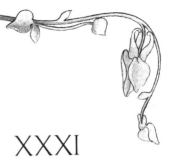

XXXI

Thou comest! all is said without a word.
I sit beneath thy looks, as children do
In the noon-sun, with souls that tremble through
Their happy eyelids from an unaverred
Yet prodigal inward joy. Behold, I erred
In that last doubt! and yet I cannot rue
The sin most, but the occasion . . . that we two
Should for a moment stand unministered
By a mutual presence. Ah, keep near and close,
Thou dovelike help! and, when my fears would rise,
With thy broad heart serenely interpose:
Brood down with thy divine sufficiencies
These thoughts which tremble when bereft of those,
Like callow birds left desert to the skies.

XXXII

The first time that the sun rose on thine oath
To love me, I looked forward to the moon
To slacken all those bonds which seemed too soon
And quickly tied to make a lasting troth.
Quick-loving hearts, I thought, may quickly loathe;
And, looking on myself, I seemed not one
For such man's love!—more like an out-of-tune
Worn viol, a good singer would be wroth
To spoil his song with, and which, snatched in haste,
Is laid down at the first ill-sounding note.
I did not wrong myself so, but I placed
A wrong on *thee*. For perfect strains may float
'Neath master-hands from instruments defaced,—
And great souls, at one stroke, may do and dote.

XXXIII

Yes, call me by my pet name! let me hear
The name I used to run at, when a child,
From innocent play, and leave the cowslips piled,
To glance up in some face that proved me dear
With the look of its eyes. I miss the clear
Fond voices which, being drawn and reconciled
Into the music of Heaven's undefiled,
Call me no longer. Silence on the bier,
While I call God . . . call God!—so let thy mouth
Be heir to those who are now exanimate.
Gather the north flowers to complete the south,
And catch the early love up in the late.
Yes, call me by that name,—and I, in truth,
With the same heart, will answer and not wait.

XXXIV

With the same heart, I said, I'll answer thee
As those, when thou shalt call me by my name—
Lo, the vain promise! is the same, the same,
Perplexed and ruffled by life's strategy?
When called before, I told how hastily
I dropped my flowers or brake off from a game,
To run and answer with the smile that came
At play last moment, and went on with me
Through my obedience. When I answer now,
I drop a grave thought, break from solitude;
Yet still my heart goes to thee—ponder how—
Not as to a single good, but all my good!
Lay thy hand on it, best one, and allow
That no child's foot could run fast as this blood.

XXXV

If I leave all for thee, wilt thou exchange
And be all to me? Shall I never miss
Home-talk and blessing and the common kiss
That comes to each in turn, nor count it strange,
When I look up, to drop on a new range
Of walls and floors, . . . another home than this?
Nay, wilt thou fill that place by me which is
Filled by dead eyes too tender to know change?
That's hardest. If to conquer love, has tried,
To conquer grief, tries more, as all things prove,
For grief indeed is love and grief beside.
Alas, I have grieved so I am hard to love.
Yet love me—wilt thou? Open thine heart wide,
And fold within, the wet wings of thy dove.

XXXVI

When we first met and loved, I did not build
Upon the event with marble. Could it mean
To last, a love set pendulous between
Sorrow and sorrow? Nay, I rather thrilled,
Distrusting every light that seemed to gild
The onward path, and feared to overlean
A finger even. And, though I have grown serene
And strong since then, I think that God has willed
A still renewable fear . . . O love, O troth . . .
Lest these enclaspèd hands should never hold,
This mutual kiss drop down between us both
As an unowned thing, once the lips being cold,
And Love be false! if *he,* to keep one oath,
Must lose one joy, by his life's star foretold.

XXXVII

Pardon, oh, pardon, that my soul should make
Of all that strong divineness which I know
For thine and thee, an image only so
Formed of the sand, and fit to shift and break.
It is that distant years which did not take
Thy sovranty, recoiling with a blow,
Have forced my swimming brains to undergo
Their doubt and dread, and blindly to forsake
Thy purity of likeness and distort
Thy worthiest love to a worthless counterfeit.
As if a shipwrecked Pagan, safe in port,
His guardian sea god to commemorate,
Should set a sculptured porpoise, gills a-snort
And vibrant tail, within the temple gate.

XXXVIII

First time he kissed me, he but only kissed
The fingers of this hand wherewith I write;
And ever since, it grew more clean and white, . . .
Slow to world-greetings, quick with its "Oh, list,"
When the angels speak. A ring of amethyst
I could not wear here, plainer to my sight,
Than that first kiss. The second passed in height
The first, and sought the forehead, and half missed,
Half falling on the hair. O beyond meed!
That was the chrism of love, which love's own crown,
With sanctifying sweetness, did precede.
The third upon my lips was folded down
In perfect, purple state; since when, indeed,
I have been proud and said, "My love, my own."

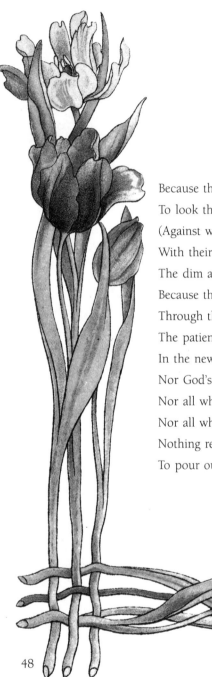

XXXIX

Because thou hast the power and own'st the grace
To look through and behind this mask of me,
(Against which, years have beat thus blanchingly
With their rains,) and behold my soul's true face,
The dim and weary witness of life's race,—
Because thou hast the faith and love to see,
Through that same soul's distracting lethargy,
The patient angel waiting for a place
In the new heavens!—because nor sin nor woe,
Nor God's infliction, nor death's neighborhood,
Nor all which others viewing, turn to go, . . .
Nor all which makes me tired of all, self-viewed, . .
Nothing repels thee, . . . Dearest, teach me so
To pour out gratitude, as thou dost, good.

XL

Oh, yes! they love through all this world of ours!
I will not gainsay love, called love forsooth.
I have heard love talked in my early youth,
And since, not so long back but that the flowers
Then gathered, smell still. Mussulmans and Giaours
Throw kerchiefs at a smile, and have no ruth
For any weeping. Polypheme's white tooth
Slips on the nut if, after frequent showers,
The shell is over-smooth,—and not so much
Will turn the thing called love, aside to hate
Or else to oblivion. But thou art not such
A lover, my Belovèd! thou canst wait
Through sorrow and sickness, to bring souls to touch,
And think it soon when others cry "Too late."

XLI

I thank all who have loved me in their hearts,
With thanks and love from mine. Deep thanks to all
Who paused a little near the prison wall
To hear my music in its louder parts
Ere they went onward, each one to the mart's
Or temple's occupation, beyond call.
But thou, who, in my voice's sink and fall
When the sob took it, thy divinest Art's
Own instrument didst drop down at thy foot
To hearken what I said between my tears, . . .
Instruct me how to thank thee!—Oh, to shoot
My soul's full meaning into future years,
That *they* should lend it utterance, and salute
Love that endures, from Life that disappears!

XLII

"My future will not copy fair my past"—
I wrote that once; and thinking at my side
My ministering life-angel justified
The word by his appealing look upcast
To the white throne of God, I turned at last,
And there, instead, saw thee, not unallied
To angels in thy soul! Then I, long tried
By natural ills, received the comfort fast,
While budding, at thy sight, my pilgrim's staff
Gave out green leaves with morning dews
   impearled.
I seek no copy now of life's first half:
Leave here the pages with long musing curled,
And write me new my future's epigraph,
New angel mine, unhoped for in the world!

XLIII

How do I love thee? Let me count the ways.
I love thee to the depth and breadth and height
My soul can reach, when feeling out of sight
For the ends of Being and ideal Grace.
I love thee to the level of everyday's
Most quiet need, by sun and candlelight.
I love thee freely, as men strive for Right;
I love thee purely, as they turn from Praise.
I love thee with the passion put to use
In my old griefs, and with my childhood's faith.
I love thee with a love I seemed to lose
With my lost saints,—I love thee with the breath,
Smiles, tears, of all my life!—and, if God choose,
I shall but love thee better after death.

XLIV

Belovèd, thou hast brought me many flowers
Plucked in the garden, all the summer through
And winter, and it seemed as if they grew
In their close room, nor missed the sun and showers.
So, in the like name of that love of ours,
Take back these thoughts which here unfolded too,
And which on warm and cold days I withdrew
From my heart's ground. Indeed, those beds
    and bowers
Be overgrown with bitter weeds and rue,
And wait thy weeding; yet here's eglantine,
Here's ivy!—take them, as I used to do
Thy flowers, and keep them where they shall not pine.
Instruct thine eyes to keep their colors true,
And tell thy soul, their roots are left in mine.

OTHER LOVE POEMS

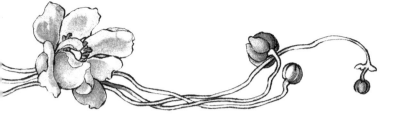

LOVE

We cannot live, except thus mutually
We alternate, aware or unaware,
The reflex act of life: and when we bear
Our virtue onward most impulsively,
Most full of invocation, and to be
Most instantly compellant, certes, there
We live most life, whoever breathes most air
And counts his dying years by sun and sea.
But when a soul, by choice and conscience, doth
Throw out her full force on another soul,
The conscience and the concentration both
Make mere life, Love. For Life in perfect whole
And aim consummated, is Love in sooth,
As nature's magnet-heat rounds pole with pole.

THE LADY'S YES

I

"Yes," I answered you last night;
   "No," this morning, sir, I say.
Colors seen by candlelight
   Will not look the same by day.

II

When the viols played their best,
   Lamps above and laughs below,
Love me sounded like a jest,
   Fit for *yes* or fit for *no.*

III

Call me false or call me free—
   Vow, whatever light may shine,
No man on your face shall see
   Any grief for change on mine.

IV

Yet the sin is on us both;
   Time to dance is not to woo;
Wooing light makes fickle troth,
   Scorn of *me* recoils on *you.*

V

Learn to win a lady's faith
   Nobly as the thing is high,
Bravely, as for life and death—
   With a loyal gravity.

VI

Lead her from the festive boards,
   Point her to the starry skies;
Guard her, by your truthful words,
   Pure from courtship's flatteries.

VII

By your truth she shall be true,
    Ever true, as wives of yore;
And her *yes,* once said to you,
    SHALL be Yes for evermore.

QUESTION AND
ANSWER

I

Love you seek for, presupposes
    Summer heat and sunny glow.
Tell me, do you find moss roses
    Budding, blooming in the snow?
Snow might kill the rose tree's root—
Shake it quickly from your foot,
    Lest it harm you as you go.

II

From the ivy where it dapples
    A gray ruin, stone by stone,—
Do you look for grapes or apples,
    Or for sad green leaves alone?
Pluck the leaves off, two or three—
Keep them for morality
    When you shall be safe and gone.

PROOF AND
DISPROOF

I

Dost thou love me, my Belovèd?
  Who shall answer yes or no?
What is provèd or disprovèd
  When my soul inquireth so,
Dost thou love me, my Belovèd?

II

I have seen thy heart today,
  Never open to the crowd,
While to love me aye and aye
  Was the vow as it was vowed
By thine eyes of steadfast gray.

III

Now I sit alone, alone—
  And the hot tears break and burn,
Now, Belovèd, thou art gone,
  Doubt and terror have their turn.
Is it love that I have known?

IV

I have known some bitter things,—
   Anguish, anger, solitude.
Year by year an evil brings,
   Year by year denies a good;
March winds violate my springs.

V

I have known how sickness bends,
   I have known how sorrow breaks,—
How quick hopes have sudden ends,
   How the heart thinks till it aches
Of the smile of buried friends.

VI

Last, I have known *thee,* my brave
   Noble thinker, lover, doer!
The best knowledge last I have.
   But thou comest as the thrower
Of fresh flowers upon a grave.

VII

Count what feelings used to move me!
   Can this love assort with those?
Thou, who art so far above me,
   Wilt thou stoop so, for repose?
Is it true that thou canst love me?

VIII

Do not blame me if I doubt thee.
   I can call love by its name
When thine arm is wrapt about me;
   But even love seems not the same,
When I sit alone, without thee.

A VALEDICTION

God be with thee my beloved,—God be with thee!
  Else alone thou goest forth,
  Thy face unto the north,
Moor and pleasance all around thee and beneath thee
  Looking equal in one snow!
  While I try to reach thee,
  Vainly follow, vainly follow,
  With the farewell and the hollo,
  And cannot reach thee so.
  Alas! I can but teach thee.
God be with thee my beloved,—God be with thee!

Can I teach thee, my beloved—can I teach thee?
  If I said, Go left or right,
  The counsel would be light,
The wisdom, poor of all that could enrich thee!
  My right would show like left;
  My raising would depress thee,
  My choice of light would blind thee,
  Of way, would leave behind thee,
  Of end, would leave bereft!
  Alas! I can but bless thee—
May God teach thee my beloved,—may God teach thee!

Can I bless thee, my beloved,—can I bless thee?
   What blessing word can I,
   From mine own tears, keep dry?
What flowers grow in my field wherewith to dress thee?
   My good reverts to ill;
   My calmnesses would move thee,
   My softnesses would prick thee,
   My bindings up would break thee,
   My crownings, curse and kill.
   Alas! I can but love thee.
May God bless thee my beloved,—may God bless thee!

Can I love thee, my beloved,—can I love thee?
   And is this like love, to stand
   With no help in my hand,
When strong as death I fain would watch above thee?
   My love-kiss can deny
   No tears that fall beneath it:
   Mine oath of love can swear thee
   From no ill that comes near thee,—
   And thou diest while I breathe it,
   And I—*I* can but die!
May God love thee my beloved,—may God love thee!

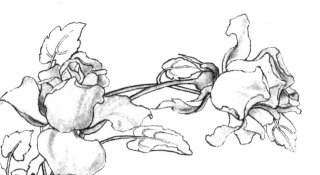

LIFE AND LOVE

I

Fast this Life of mine was dying,
  Blind already and calm as death,
Snowflakes on her bosom lying
  Scarcely heaving with her breath.

II

Love came by, and having known her
  In a dream of fabled lands,
Gently stooped, and laid upon her
  Mystic chrism of holy hands;

III

Drew his smile across her folded
  Eyelids, as the swallow dips;
Breathed as finely as the cold did
  Through the locking of her lips.

IV

So, when Life looked upward, being
  Warmed and breathed on from above,
What sight could she have for seeing,
  Evermore . . . but only Love?